Contents

Written by
Alison Hawes

Illustrated by
Ollie Cuthbertson

Series editor **Dee Reid**

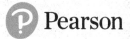 **Pearson**

Characters

King Arik

Haldor

Larvig

King Surl

The troll

The troll's mother

New vocabulary

ch1	p3	warriors
ch1	p5	favour
ch2	p8	massive
ch2	p9	spurted

ch3	p12	towering
ch3	p14	slumped
ch3	p14	slunk

Introduction

Haldor, son of King Arik, is a warrior. Arik receives a message from the nearby kingdom of King Surl. A huge troll is attacking King Surl's people. Arik must choose a brave warrior to cross the sea to kill the troll. He chooses his only son, Haldor.

Haldor and the Troll

Chapter One

One frosty evening, King Arik called his warriors to his Great Hall. He stood in front of them and said, "I have had a message from King Surl. Every night a huge troll is attacking his people. Tomorrow I will send one of you across the sea to rid King Surl of this beast."

All the warriors stood tall. Each man hoped that he would be chosen by Arik to kill the troll. Then Arik put his hand on his son's shoulder. He said, "If you agree, I will choose my son, Haldor, to kill the troll. His friend, Larvig, will go with him."

But when the other warriors heard this, they were jealous.

"Arik shows too much favour to his son," whispered one warrior.

"There are older warriors who have fought trolls before. They should be chosen, not Haldor," said another warrior. "We should not allow this."

"Wait!" whispered another warrior. "I have heard of this troll. Everyone who has fought it has died."

"Then let us agree to Haldor going," grinned another, "and we will never have to see him again!"

"We agree that you should send Haldor!" roared the warriors.

Chapter Two

Haldor and Larvig set off in their dragon boat for King Surl's kingdom. King Surl greeted Haldor and Larvig with open arms. That night, Haldor stayed in the king's Great Hall on his own, to fight the troll alone.

It was just getting dark when the hall door burst open and a huge one-eyed troll appeared.

With one sweep of its massive claw, the troll scooped Haldor off the floor. Haldor bit hard into the troll's rough flesh and, just for a second, the troll let go slightly. It was all that Haldor needed.

He jumped on to the troll's shoulders and twisted one of its arms behind its back. Then, with a mighty roar, he tore the troll's arm off at the shoulder. Blood spurted on to the floor and, with a howl, the troll staggered out into the snow to die.

King Surl held a great feast in Haldor's honour.

"You have brought peace to this land," he said.

"Our days of terror are over."

That night Haldor heard terrible screams. It was the troll's mother crying as she held her dead son in her arms. When Haldor heard those screams he knew it was not the end.

Chapter Three

In the middle of the night, the hall door crashed open. The sleeping warriors woke up to find the troll's mother towering above them. Her clothes were covered with the blood of her son.

"A life for a life!" she screamed, snatching up the nearest warrior in her claws.

Haldor sprang to his feet. It was Larvig who the troll held in her massive claws. Larvig struggled but the more he struggled, the tighter the troll held him in her grasp.

"Spare my friend's life," shouted Haldor. "He did not kill your son. I did."

The troll turned to face Haldor. For a moment, she gave him a cold, one-eyed stare. Then, dropping Larvig, she grabbed Larvig's sword and threw it hard at Haldor. There was the sound of metal cutting through flesh and bone as Haldor slumped to the floor.

"Your life for my son's life!" she cried.

Then she slunk out into the snow, bending her body against the howling wind.

Larvig rushed to Haldor's side. Blood was flowing from a wound deep in his chest.

"Help me stop the bleeding," said Haldor. "Then I must find the troll's cave and finish the task I was sent to do."

Chapter Four

In the moonlight, Haldor could see a trail of blood in the snow. It led him to the troll's cave. Haldor could hear the troll sobbing as she held her dead son in her arms.

"Killer!" she screamed when she saw Haldor, and grabbed a giant sword off the wall. She rushed at Haldor, swinging the sword at his head. Haldor's chest hurt but he dodged the sword and flung the troll hard against the cave wall. Her sword fell to the floor.

Haldor sprinted across the cave and lifted the giant sword with both his hands. Then, with a mighty roar, he chopped the troll's head from her shoulders.

Some days later, Haldor's dragon boat sailed home. Arik and his men went down to meet it. As Haldor and Larvig came ashore, Haldor stepped forward and placed his hand on his father's shoulder.

"I am glad to be home," he said.

"And you return a hero!" said Arik.

Then Haldor turned and faced his father's warriors.

He threw a bag at their feet.

"A gift for those men who thought my father had

chosen the wrong warrior," he shouted as the

troll's head rolled out of the bag on to the snow.

Quiz

Text comprehension

Literal comprehension
p5 Why were the other warriors jealous?
p13 Who is the troll's mother holding in her claws?
p18 How did Haldor kill the troll's mother?

Inferential comprehension
p12 What does the mother mean by 'A life for a life'?
p13 How can you tell Haldor is a true friend?
p20 How did Haldor treat his father's warriors?

Personal response
- Would you have wanted to have been chosen to fight the troll?
- Would you have been jealous that King Arik chose his son?
- Do you feel sorry for the troll's mother?

Author's style

p6 Find three speech verbs on this page.
p7 How does the author build up tension in the final sentence?
p8 Which adjectives and verbs does the author use in the first two sentences to describe the size of the troll.

Before reading A Life for a Life

Characters

- **King Surl**
- **Troll**
- **Haldor** (a brave warrior)
- **Larvig** (Haldor's friend)

Setting the scene

Haldor has killed the one-eyed troll that has been attacking King Surl's kingdom for years. But the next night, while King Surl and his warriors are asleep in the Great Hall, the mother of the dead troll comes bursting into the hall. She is seeking revenge for her son's death.

King Surl: How dare you come here? You and your son have killed hundreds of my people.

Troll: And now my son is lying dead in the snow. One of you killed him.

Haldor: Your son was a cruel killer.

King Surl: Now he is dead and my people are safe at last.

Troll: I will not leave this place until I have killed the man who killed my son.

Haldor: Your son showed no mercy to the people he killed when he burst into this hall looking for his next victim.

Larvig: He tore them to pieces and he drank their blood.

Troll: He was my only son. He was all I had in the world!

King Surl: My son is also dead. While he was sleeping in the forest your son split his head open and then beat him to a pulp with a mace.

Troll: I do not care about your son. Someone must pay for my son's life with their life. A life for a life!

King Surl: But you and I are old now. We have seen so much death and fighting. Let's end all this killing now.

Troll: Never! Not while I am alive!

Haldor: Then you will die too.

Troll: This warrior will be the first to die. I will tear off his arms.

Larvig: Let me go!

Haldor: It was not Larvig who killed your son. It was me and now I will kill you.

Larvig: Take care, Haldor. She has let me go but she has my sword.

Troll: First I will scrape off your face with my claws and then I will kill you with this sword.

Haldor: You'll have to catch me first!

Larvig: Run, Haldor!

Troll: You cannot run from me. Feel this cold metal through your flesh and bones. *(She throws the sword at Haldor and it hits his chest.)* I will leave you to die a slow death!

Larvig: The troll has stabbed Haldor with my sword. Help me stop the blood.

King Surl: Will he live?

Larvig: The wound is deep but Haldor is strong. He will live.

Haldor: Help me up. I must find the troll and kill her.

King Surl: When will all this killing end?

Larvig: Haldor must finish what his father sent him to do.

Haldor: Then at last there will be peace.

Quiz

Text comprehension

p24 How did the troll kill King Surl's son?

p24 What arguments does King Surl give for stopping the quarrel with the troll?

p27 How can you tell that the troll is cruel?

Vocabulary

p23 Find an adjective meaning 'causing pain and suffering'.

p23 Find a word meaning 'pity' or 'kindness'.

p23 Find a phrase meaning 'breaking off someone's limbs'.

Before reading ᴜᴘ ʜᴇʟʟʏ ᴀᴀ

Find out about

- The Up Helly Aa festival held every year in the Shetland Islands.

New vocabulary

p31 raided	**p34** celebrate
p31 settle	**p36** costumes

Introduction

Hundreds of years ago, Vikings from Norway came to the Shetland Islands. Today, the people of the Shetland Islands remember their Viking history in a festival called Up Helly Aa. Every year the people dress as Vikings and pull a dragon ship through the town. Then, at night, they set fire to the ship.

Up Helly Aa

Raiders and Settlers

Hundreds of years ago, Vikings from Norway raided other countries for gold and slaves. But not all Vikings came to raid. Some came to find new lands to settle and live in.

The Shetland Islands

Some Vikings came to live in the Shetland Islands in Scotland.

Viking settlers built stone buildings.

Vikings Rule!

Viking names

Many family names and names of places in the Shetland Islands are Viking names. This is not surprising, as the Vikings ruled the Shetland Islands for 600 years! Did you know that these are all Viking words?

- egg
- sister
- leg
- knife
- sky
- window

Festival

Today, the people of the Shetland Islands remember their Viking history in a festival called Up Helly Aa. The Up Helly Aa festival began in the 1880s and it takes place every year.

The Islanders dressed as Vikings.

Up Helly Aa

Fire festival

Up Helly Aa began as a fire festival to celebrate the end of the long winter days. Over the years, the festival has changed. Now it also celebrates the islands' Viking history but fire is still an important part of the modern Up Helly Aa festival. Each year, on the last Tuesday in January, hundreds of people take part in the festival and thousands come to watch. The festival lasts all day and all night!

On the Day

The march

Up Helly Aa day begins with a march through the town. Men dressed as Vikings carry axes and shields as they march through the streets.

In Secret

For months the people of the Shetland Islands have secretly been making costumes, torches and a Viking dragon ship. Now the waiting is over. As part of the march, the ship is pulled through the streets for everyone to see.

The dragon was used to frighten sea monsters.

On the Night

Torches

When it is dark, hundreds of torches are lit.
Then hundreds of people carry the burning
torches to the place where the dragon ship
will be burned.

Dragon ship

When they arrive at the place where the ship is to be burned, the torches are thrown on to the ship. Then the people sing as the dragon ship goes up in flames. After the burning of the ship there is dancing and singing at halls in the town. This goes on long into the night so the day after Up Helly Aa is a holiday in the Shetland Islands!

Quiz

Text comprehension

Literal comprehension
p31 Did all Viking invaders come to raid?

p32 What is the evidence that Vikings once ruled the Shetland Islands?

p33 When did the Up Helly Aa festival begin?

Inferential comprehension
p34 Why is fire an important part of the festival?

p36 Why are the costumes and the dragon ship made in secret?

p38 Why is the day after Up Helly Aa a holiday?

Personal response
- Would you like to dress up as a Viking warrior and march through the streets?
- Do you go to any festivals during the year? What does the festival celebrate?
- Would you be interested in going to the Up Helly Aa festival? Why?

Non-fiction features

p32 Why are bullet points used on this page?

p36 What is the caption on this page?

p38 If you were presenting this information in bullet points, where would you put the bullet points?

Published by Pearson Education Limited, Edinburgh Gate, Harlow, Essex, CM20 2JE.

www.pearsonschoolsandfecolleges.co.uk

Text © Pearson Education Limited 2012

Edited by Jo Dilloway
Designed by Tony Richardson and Siu Hang Wong
Original illustrations © Pearson Education Limited 2012
Illustrated by Ollie Cuthbertson
Cover design by Siu Hang Wong
Picture research by Melissa Allison
Cover illustration © Pearson Education Limited 2012

The right of Alison Hawes to be identified as author of this work has been asserted by her in
accordance with the Copyright, Designs and Patents Act 1988.

First published 2012

25
16

British Library Cataloguing in Publication Data
A catalogue record for this book is available from the British Library

ISBN 978 0 435 07097 7

Printed and bound in Great Britain by Bell and Bain Ltd, Glasgow

Acknowledgements
The author and publisher would like to thank the following individuals and organisations for permission
to reproduce photographs:

(Key: b-bottom; c-centre; l-left; r-right; t-top)

Alamy Images: Dave Donaldson 36, 38, Roger Cracknell 01 / Classic 32–33; Getty Images: Jeff J
Mitchell 37r, Workbook Stock 31; Press Association Images: PA Archive / Andrew Milligan 1, 34–35,
PA Archive / Danny Lawson 37l

Cover images: Back: Press Association Images: PA Archive / Danny Lawson

All other images © Pearson Education

Every effort has been made to contact copyright holders of material reproduced in this book. Any
omissions will be rectified in subsequent printings if notice is given to the publishers.